DATE DUE

WILDERNESS RESCUE WITH THE U.S. SEARCH AND RESCUE TASK FORCE

Rescue and Prevention: Defending Our Nation

- Biological and Germ Warfare Protection
- Border and Immigration Control
- Counterterrorist Forces with the CIA
- The Department of Homeland Security
- The Drug Enforcement Administration
- Firefighters
- Hostage Rescue with the FBI
- The National Guard
- Police Crime Prevention
- Protecting the Nation with the U.S. Air Force
- Protecting the Nation with the U.S. Army
- Protecting the Nation with the U.S. Navy
- Rescue at Sea with the U.S. and Canadian Coast Guards
- The U.S. Transportation Security Administration
- Wilderness Rescue with the U.S. Search and Rescue Task Force

WILDERNESS RESCUE WITH THE U.S. SEARCH AND RESCUE TASK FORCE

BRENDA RALPH LEWIS

MASON CREST PUBLISHERS
www.masoncrest.com

Mason Crest Publishers Inc.
370 Reed Road
Broomall, PA 19008
(866) MCP-BOOK (toll free)
www.masoncrest.com

First printing

1 2 3 4 5 6 7 8 9 10

Library of Congress Cataloging-in-Publication Data on file
at the Library of Congress

ISBN 1-59084-404-1

Editorial and design by
Amber Books Ltd.
Bradley's Close
74–77 White Lion Street
London N1 9PF
www.amberbooks.co.uk

Project Editor: Michael Spilling
Design: Graham Curd
Picture Research: Natasha Jones

Printed and bound in Jordan

Picture credits
Corbis: 81; Federal Emergency Management Agency: 19, 20, 21, 27, 63, 71, 80, 86; Popperfoto: 6, 11, 15, 33, 42, 48, 53, 56, 57, 59, 61, 62, 64, 67, 69, 78, 82, 85; Topham Picturepoint: 8, 10, 13, 14, 17, 24, 26, 29, 30, 32, 34, 37, 41, 51, 68, 75, 77, 84; U.S. Coast Guard: 22, 38, 44, 55; U.S. Department of Defense: 36, 47, 50, 72, 74, 88.
Front cover: Topham Picturepoint; USSARTF (center).

DEDICATION

This book is dedicated to those who perished in the terrorist attacks of September 11, 2001, and to all the committed individuals who continually serve to defend freedom and protect the American people.

CONTENTS

INTRODUCTION

September 11, 2001, saw terrorism cast its lethal shadow across the globe. The deaths inflicted at the Twin Towers, at the Pentagon, and in Pennsylvania were truly an attack on the world and civilization itself. However, even as the impact echoed around the world, the forces of decency were fighting back: Americans drew inspiration from a new breed of previously unsung, everyday heroes. Amid the smoking rubble, firefighters, police officers, search-and-rescue, and other "first responders" made history. The sacrifices made that day will never be forgotten.

Out of the horror and destruction, we have fought back on every front. When the terrorists struck, their target was not just the United States, but also the values that the American people share with others all over the world who cherish freedom. Country by country, region by region, state by state, we have strengthened our public-safety efforts to make it much more difficult for terrorists.

Others have come to the forefront: from the Coast Guard to the Border Patrol, a wide range of agencies work day and night for our protection. Before the terrorist attacks of September 11, 2001, launched them into the spotlight, the courage of these guardians went largely unrecognized, although in truth, the sense of service was always honor enough for them. We can never repay the debt we owe them, but by increasing our understanding of the work they do, the *Rescue and Prevention: Defending Our Nation* books will enable us to better appreciate our brave defenders.

Steven L. Labov—CISM, MSO, CERT 3
Chief of Department, United States Search and Rescue Task Force

Left: Here, doctors and rescue workers in the Swiss Alps administer first aid to the victim of an avalanche.

SURVIVING IN THE WILDERNESS

What is a wilderness? And why are there so many search-and-rescue (SAR) services around the world to help people who get into trouble while they are there? The word itself provides the answer.

"Wilderness" comes from a combination of "wild" and "deor," which is Old English for "beast" or "deer," suggesting that it originally described a place where wild animals lived. Of course, not every wilderness contains wild animals, but there are plenty of other problems.

It is difficult to survive in the wilderness. You must do everything for yourself—supply your own food and equipment, and your own shelter to sleep in at night or to protect you against bad weather. This is a place where nature rules, and nature is not always friendly. Storms or floods are nature in a bad mood. Sunshine may seem like nature in a good mood, but it burns the skin, and its heat can kill you or make you feel very ill by **dehydrating** your body; and if the weather becomes too cold, your body temperature can drop to an alarmingly low level and you may get hypothermia. Whatever the conditions, you are in great danger.

Left: Climbing a vertical wall of ice in the Adirondack Mountains, New York State. Note the long safety rope attached to the climber to catch him if he falls.

The wild, open spaces of the wilderness are tempting for people who live with the rush and crush of cities.

CITY LIFE

Despite these risks, many people choose to go into the wilderness during their vacations. One reason is that modern life in the cities can be stressful. People want to escape from the noise, the crowds, the rush, and the traffic of city life and spend time in a more peaceful environment. Some of them trek across deserts or **scrubland**; some climb mountains or explore caves; others love to camp out in the wide open spaces of wilderness country and "sleep under the stars," just as people did in ancient times.

Whatever they do, their purpose is the same: to get "close to nature," which is definitely not something you can do in a city. To live for a while in the wilderness, far from buildings, roads, or

It is a tough existence, living in the Indian desert state of Rajasthan. Here, a Rajasthani nomad prepares a meal outdoors. However, it is often the challenge of harsh and difficult conditions that attract urban dwellers to venture into wild regions.

SEARCH AND RESCUE AROUND THE WORLD

There are search-and-rescue organizations in many countries, large and small, across the world. Here are some of them:

Australia:
Queensland Rescue
Victoria State Emergency Service
Bushwhackers Rescue Group

Great Britain:
Mountain Rescue Council

Canada:
Search and Rescue Society of British Columbia
Canadian Avalanche Association
Surrey Search and Rescue Society
Wilderness Search and Rescue Association (NAWSAR)

Europe:
International Commission for Alpine Rescue (Austria, France, Germany, Switzerland)

Finland:
Helikopterpalvelu Search and Rescue, which uses (as the name suggests) helicopters

Ireland:
Irish Mountain Rescue Association

Nepal:
Himalayan Rescue Association

New Zealand:
New Zealand Land and Sea Rescue

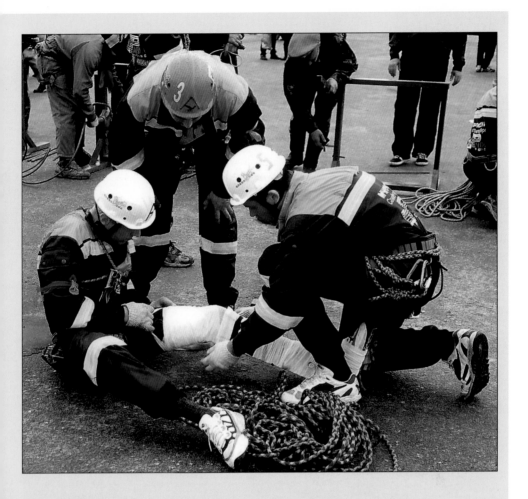

Here, Russian search-and-rescue teams participate in a contest to demonstrate their skills in the Russian Emergency Situations Ministry, Moscow, in 2000.

United States:
Search and Rescue Task Force (USSARTF)
Mountain Rescue Association (MAR)
Rocky Mountain Rescue Group
Sheriffs' Search and Rescue Team (California)

Showing the simple life in the "great outdoors," Native American women cook a meal over a fire in Monument Valley, Arizona.

people, is most definitely therapeutic. In the past, and even today, people did not regard the wilderness as a place for a vacation: it was their home. Nomadic Arabs lived in the sand-and-rock deserts of the Middle East; Native Americans lived on the Great Plains of the western United States; Aborigines knew how to survive in the wilds of the Australian **outback**.

LIVING IN THE WILDERNESS

It is important to recognize the difference between these people and city dwellers who visit the wilderness for a short while. The wilderness dwellers never lived any other way. They had the knowledge, passed down to them by their ancestors, how to survive in inhospitable places. They could "read" the wilderness, track animals, follow trails, and interpret sounds and smells. They could recognize and use healing herbs and roots, and knew which plants or berries they could safely eat and which were poisonous to them.

Helicopters play a vital part in wilderness rescue, enabling medical teams like this one to reach the scene of an emergency and take accident victims to the nearest hospital quickly.

SNIFFING TO THE RESCUE

Search-and-rescue teams often use dogs because of their wonderful sense of smell. People and animals leave a scent wherever they go. People do not notice this scent, but dogs pick it up easily.

Dogs pick up the scent of a missing person by being given one of the person's belongings, probably a piece of clothing, to sniff. Then, they are off—noses to the ground—following that scent, sometimes over long distances; other scents rarely confuse them.

In 1996, a Labrador called Fergus tracked down a hunter missing in Montana. It was winter, with a lot of snow and ice on the ground, and the rescuers were worried that the man would freeze to death if he was not found by nightfall. He was ill-equipped to survive, having no map, no warm clothing, and no matches to light a fire.

Fergus got to work. She led her handler and the rest of the search team over a meadow, along mountain ridges, and through a forest, where the man's footprints could just be made out in the snow. After traveling further, members of the search team found a man sheltering in a cabin. Was he the missing hunter? Fergus soon showed the team that he was. Arriving at the cabin where he was standing with members of the search team, Fergus went straight up to the man she had been seeking to identify him. Good search-and-rescue dogs can save lives in such situations.

Once people began to live in towns and cities, around 6,000 years ago, they had no need to do any of this any more. As the centuries passed, they lost the ability to survive in the wilderness. After all, why go out and trap your own food if you can buy it? Why bother with difficult treks through the wilderness when you can travel easily by horse, carriage, train, or car? Why look for healing herbs if you can ask a doctor for medicine or take a bandage from the medicine cabinet?

Of course, people in the wilderness do not have to go without bandages or medicines; they can take them along, together with

A trainee avalanche rescue team—a trainer and his dog—dig a "victim" out of the snow in the Colorado Mountains.

their food and other supplies. If things go according to plan, they are unlikely to need them. But what if things go wrong? What if they are trapped by floods, mudslides, or an avalanche of snow? What if they get hurt in a rockfall? What if they slip on wet rocks while crossing a river? What if they fall ill?

Too many people in situations like this lack the knowledge to get out of trouble on their own. Today, however, the dangers of the wilderness are recognized and, as a result, there are now many SAR services that can seek and find people who need help and give medical treatment if needed.

SAR VOLUNTEERS

The work of the search-and-rescue services is skillful, and often **altruistic**. Many rescuers are volunteers, donating their time and money to help their fellow human beings in trouble. As Richard Sale of the U.S. Sierra Madre Search and Rescue Group put it, "We'll go any place, at any time, to help anyone, for no charge."

The same idea lies behind the mottoes that some SAR organizations choose to set out their beliefs. For instance, the United States Search and Rescue Task Force (USSARTF) has "Working Together So Others May Live"; the New Zealand Land and Search Rescue has "Volunteers Serving the Community."

The people who belong to SAR organizations must be serious and dedicated to their task. After all, they do not work normal office hours: search and rescue continues 24 hours a day, 7 days a week. For them, there is no question of going home at the end of the working day and returning to the office the next morning.

NOT JUST WILDERNESS RESCUE:
THE WORK OF THE USSARTF

The U.S. Search and Rescue Task
Force, a volunteer group formed in
1999, operates over a wide area of
the eastern United States:
Pennsylvania, New Jersey, New York,
Delaware, Maryland, Virginia, West
Virginia, and the District of Columbia.
In addition, the Task Force is willing to go
to the rescue anywhere in the United States.

In its short existence, it has been almost too successful: "We
hadn't meant to go beyond our first or second state for five years,
until 2004," explains Steven Labov, the Task Force Chief. "So we're
way ahead of schedule!"

The USSARTF does a lot more than rescue people from the
wilderness. It also carries out urban searches, looking for victims in
collapsed buildings, tracking criminals, finding lost children, and
rescuing animals, as well as people, trapped by disasters such as
fires or floods. In addition, the USSARTF runs classes to teach
people about the dangers they can face out in the wilderness and
the ways in which they can help themselves out of trouble.

"We'd love to put ourselves out of a job," Labov remarks, "but I
don't think that will be possible. There will always be people who
get into difficulties in the wilderness and other places, so we'll
always be there to help!"

Rescuers must also train hard to keep up the skills they need for their work, and that includes making sure they know how to use the latest technology. In the 21st century, technology is advancing fast. If something new comes up that will help the work of search and rescue, then the rescuers want to know all about it. It could be a new computer system or Earth-orbiting satellite, a new use for the Internet, or a new form of transportation to get them to the rescue scene that much faster. Whatever makes search and rescue better, makes it easier to save lives.

Above and left: At Zuni in New Mexico, USSARTF firefighters take a well-earned rest from their efforts to control fires that raged across the wilderness in 2000.

GETTING READY FOR SEARCH AND RESCUE

The people who go on search-and-rescue missions in the wilderness, or anywhere else, have to be ready for action all the time, any time. They must also train and learn constantly, making sure their skills are always at their best.

The reason for this is that all SAR calls are emergencies—and, by definition, unpredictable. At any time, an SAR call may come through, alerting the team to anything—an accident, a missing person, or a group of people trapped by bad weather on a mountainside. Little wonder, then, that the USSARTF runs training courses year-round. In one six-month period, for instance, there may be as many as 34 courses, all focusing on different search and rescue subjects.

Responding to an SAR call means more than just grabbing equipment and rushing off to the rescue. A team must gather as much information in advance as possible, determining precisely where to go and how to get there, what the weather is like, how many people are in danger and need to be rescued, and whether there are any injuries requiring attention.

Particularly important is to learn how the emergency happened.

Left: This is only a practice demonstration, but it shows the dangers of rescue operations. Off the coast of Yorktown, this HH-60J U.S. Coast Guard helicopter prepares to rescue a swimmer.

Someone may have gotten into trouble while climbing a cliff in the mountains and be stuck there, unable to move either up or down; another may have gone off to explore a forest, but taken too long to return; or have fallen into a river and been swept away by the current; or slipped over in mud or on rocks, injuring a knee or an ankle and now unable to walk; or been stung by insects or bitten by snakes, both of which may require medical attention fast. Sadly, not all SAR missions have happy endings, and rescuers must accept that they may find a corpse, and not the missing person alive and well or only slightly injured.

GETTING THERE

Knowing precisely where to go on an SAR mission means that the rescuers must be familiar with the area of wilderness where the emergency happened. Just as taxi drivers should know the road system of the cities where they operate, so rescuers must know the areas in which they may be called to work. They must spend time studying maps, reading and memorizing descriptions of the area, learning from what happened on rescues elsewhere in the same region—and, most importantly, exploring the wilderness themselves. The more familiar they are in the wilderness, the better and quicker they will be able to work.

Left: Three search-and-rescue volunteers at Clark Reservation, Green Lake, Pennsylvania, help a helicopter winch up an injured man. The man can then be quickly flown to the nearest hospital for treatment.

A search-and-rescue officer scans the desert west of Tucson, Arizona. This untamed, inhospitable wilderness country is frequently used as a crossing point by illegal immigrants coming from Mexico. Some of these undocumented migrants run into trouble in the desert, and the Border Patrol has to launch rescue operations to save them from danger.

KNOWING THE WILDERNESS

Search and rescue is a job for experts, and there are many details to be learned: where the trails lead in the wilderness and whether the route will take the team over mountains, along rivers, or through woods and forests. The wilderness can be vast, so rescuers must be able to navigate over great distances, using their compasses and

THE UNITED STATES SEARCH AND RESCUE TASK FORCE OATH

Everyone who works for the USSARTF must take an oath to obey the rules of the Task Force. The oath includes these words:

"I will at no time, via direct or indirect actions, harm the reputation of the United States Search and Rescue Task Force or any of its Specialists or Officers. I...will diligently carry out the duties to which I am assigned.... I will support, obey, and uphold all of the laws of each community, state, and the United States.... I will carefully...discharge the duties of the office to which I am assigned. I will follow such orders and directions as may be given by superior officers. I shall uphold the motto of the Department: Dedication, Perseverance, Service—'Working Together, So Others May Live'."

Labrador Heidi, owner Susan Martinez (left), and Ralph Castilo of the Federal Emergency Management Agency acclimatize to wintry conditions while on a training exercise in Utah.

other direction-finding equipment to reach their destination as speedily as possible. Just as important is how they travel: some places in the wilderness can be reached overland by truck or automobile; but others may be isolated, reachable only by helicopter.

The weather in and around the wilderness must be regularly monitored. Conditions can change quickly, so that rescuers setting off in bright sunshine may arrive in the wilderness to find themselves at the center of a storm and in high winds. To anticipate weather conditions, they study long-range weather forecasts indicating possible patterns for the next few days, as well as more-detailed forecasts for the next few hours. How high or how low is the temperature? Is it going to rain? How strong are the winds blowing over the wilderness? Are there any storms heading that way? The aim is to answer as many questions as possible.

Rescuers must always make sure that they follow all necessary safety instructions. That means caring for their own safety as well as the safety of the people they are rescuing. In a mountain rescue, for example, they must be expert at using ropes, knowing the right, safe way to lower themselves down to help a climber who is stuck on a cliff. If they are saving someone from a fast-flowing river, rescuers must take care not to get swept away by the water themselves. The point is, they cannot afford mistakes: lives could be lost, and not just the lives of the people needing rescue, but their own as well.

Right: This satellite picture shows Hurricane Erin over the Atlantic on the way north to wreak havoc in areas across Virginia, Massachusetts, and Maine.

WHO ARE SEARCH AND RESCUERS?

Not everyone can be a search and rescuer. This is difficult and demanding work, and often dangerous. Rescuers must be willing not only to accept these risks, but also to do all they can to bring help. A humanitarian instinct—the simple concern for our fellow human beings—is a prerequisite.

People in difficulties, whether in the wilderness or anywhere else,

THE PHONETIC ALPHABET

A radio is one of the most valuable pieces of communication equipment for SAR teams, and rescuers must know how to use it efficiently. They learn the phonetic, or "sound," alphabet so that the messages they send to their headquarters can be clearly understood. There is no time for long explanations, and it is vital to avoid garbled messages. The phonetic alphabet guarantees that messages are understood the first time.

The phonetic system is simple. Each letter of the alphabet is represented by a word beginning with that letter: for example, Alpha for A, Delta for D, Echo for E, Yankee for Y, or Zulu for Z.

For example, to warn headquarters that there is a fire in the area, a rescuer spells it out: "Foxtrot Indigo Romeo Echo."

Left: A man is lost somewhere in the wilderness near Victory, New York State. Search-and-rescue teams relay information back to base to coordinate a successful rescue.

are usually frightened. They are in unfamiliar surroundings and afraid they may not survive. Rescuers, when they come, must provide comfort and reassurance. They have to be calm and confident, and if they have got a good sense of humor, so much the better—it helps to drive away worries. The fact that rescuers are experts at their job is also helpful; their skill inspires trust.

It is true, of course, that many people who get into difficulties

Divers from a wilderness rescue team search the river behind the home of a missing woman in Clay County, Texas. Search-and-rescue staff are often called on to help in police investigations when a person goes missing in suspicious circumstances.

have only themselves to blame. They may have tried to climb a mountain without the proper boots or equipment or ventured into the wilderness wearing unsuitable clothes or got lost because they did not have good maps or read their compass properly.

Rescuers, however, are generous people and not at all interested in assigning blame—what would be the point? As far as they are concerned, on a search-and-rescue mission, only one type of person needs help: a person in difficulty.

Search-and-rescue workers set out to search for hikers buried in an avalanche on Grouse Mountain, in British Columbia, Canada.

THE TOOLS OF SEARCH AND RESCUE

The work of search and rescue involves an enormous amount of equipment. Some of this is simple—like the ropes used in mountain rescues. Others are the result of modern technological advances—like the development of Earth-orbiting satellites.

Of great importance in search-and-rescue work are the inventions of Alexander Graham Bell and Guglielmo Marconi—namely, the telephone (invented by Bell in 1876) and the radio (Marconi sent the first radio message in 1901). Both inventions radically changed the way people were able to communicate with each other, and today's technological advances continue to do so.

The Global Positioning System (GPS) lets people pinpoint their exact location on Earth, and night-vision goggles make it possible for rescuers to see in the dark.

USING THE RADIO AND TELEPHONE

In 1901, Marconi's first radio message was heard 350 miles away. However, for many years, radio communication was interrupted by "distortion"—that is, "crackling" and other noises. Today, **VHF/FM** radios, as used by SAR teams, enable rescuers to talk over greater distances, often "bouncing" radio messages off Earth-orbiting satellites. There is little or no distortion, and every word can be heard

Left: Hard, dirty work and basic, these sandbags laid out at Oneida, New York State, are an effective defense against flooding.

Here, a U.S. Air Force officer uses a PRC-90 radio to provide coordinates for a search-and-rescue aircraft as part of a search-and-rescue training exercise in Thailand.

clearly—important in a situation in which half-heard messages or muffled words could mean the wrong information transmitted, which in turn could mean the difference between life and death for someone in trouble in the wilderness.

Also important are pagers—radio devices so small that they can be worn on a jacket or carried in a pocket. The pager beeps to indicate a message is on its way. It cannot carry a message over a long

In this illustration, a solar-powered satellite for use with the Global Positioning System is shown high above the Earth.

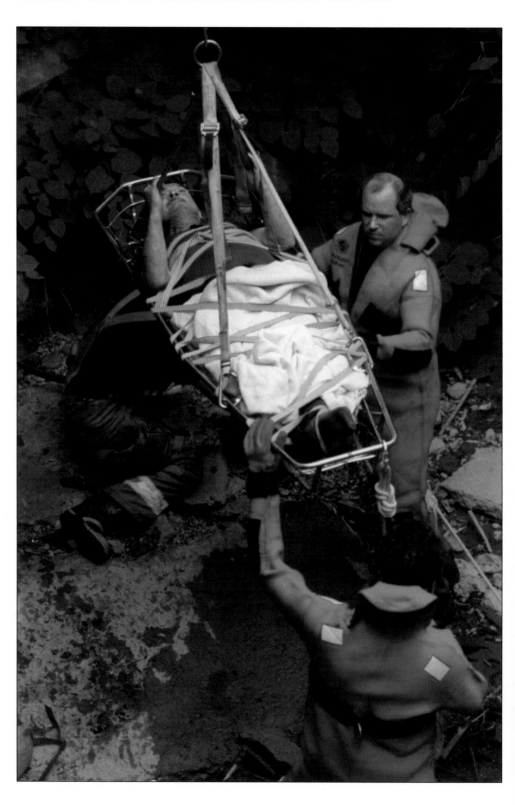

UNDERNEATH A HELICOPTER

Some search-and-rescue helicopters have sling-loading hooks. These enable large amounts of equipment—like packs, ropes, or **litters** for carrying injured people—to be placed in a sling underneath the belly of the helicopter. The sling also makes it possible to pick up loads, which are then pulled up into the helicopter and can be flown to other places where they may be needed.

distance, but is useful in situations in which rescuers may be quite close, but unable to talk to each other easily. For example, rescuers may be at different locations within the same emergency area, both giving first aid to the injured. They do not want to leave the injured person alone, so the pager enables them to pass information on or ask for advice.

Like Marconi's radio, Alexander Graham Bell's telephone has come a long way since its invention, when telephones were machines with wires and could not be moved. Today's rescuers are able to communicate by cellular phones, which are powered by batteries providing a supply of electricity, and are therefore able to be used anywhere.

Left: Matt Klicker, injured at Onondaga Creek, near Syracuse, New York State, is lifted on a rescue litter and up into a helicopter. The litter is designed to protect the injured person while offering maximum comfort.

ROPES AND KNOTS

Ropes are often used on search-and-rescue missions and, like sailors or cowboys, rescuers must learn how to knot or tie ropes so that they are strong enough for the difficult job they have to do. For example, to make a rope stronger, it can be knotted in a figure-eight shape.

Rescuers who have to rappel down a rope from a helicopter or the roof of a building often use the Prusik knot, which was named after its inventor, Dr. Karl Prusik. This is a strong knot, which can enable rescuers to climb up a rope as well as slide down it—and do it safely.

Other knots used include the double fishermen's knot, which joins two rappelling ropes safely together; the triple-loop bowline, which can be tied to make a seat-sling for someone who has been injured and needs to be lifted out of a dangerous place; or the girth hitch, which is used to tie a climbing rope to a waist harness or belt.

Right: Here, as he negotiates a dangerous waterfall, a rescuer's life hangs by a single rope—and the knots and loops that make it strong enough to hold his weight.

Computers, too, are used increasingly in search-and-rescue work—the smaller, battery-driven laptop computers can be used anywhere. A rescuer simply turns on the computer, "boots up," and within moments, is using the Internet to obtain information or send and receive e-mails.

THE GLOBAL POSITIONING SYSTEM

The Global Positioning System (**GPS**) consists of 24 satellites that orbit the Earth. These satellites send out transmissions that can be picked up by special receivers. At least four of the satellites have to be above the Earth's horizon, the line where the surface of the Earth and the sky seem to meet. Together, these four satellites work out the latitude (position north and south), the longitude (position east and west) and the altitude (height) of the receiver and, therefore, of the person using it. People lost in the wilderness, but with radio contact or other means of communication, would therefore be able to tell rescuers exactly where to find them.

Small and neat, this compass device is part of the Global Positioning System that enables visitors to the wilderness to triangulate their position on the ground.

NIGHT VISION

Even with the advantage of GPS, finding the location of a lost person is not necessarily the same thing as actually finding him. There are, for example, special difficulties if a search has to be made at night or in a dark place, such as a cave or underground mine. Fortunately, modern technology has an answer for the problem. With night-vision goggles, rescuers can see in the dark up to a distance of 200 yards (220 m). No matter how dark, no matter if the sky is full of clouds and there is no moonlight or starlight to help, the goggles let rescuers see.

How does this work? The theory behind the technology is simple. When we see objects or people, this is because of the light around them. Even in the dark, when it is almost impossible to see, there is always some light around, however little. The equipment collects these small amounts of light, including infrared light, and magnifies them. Thanks to this image enhancement, rescuers can see in the dark and operate effectively.

Another kind of night-vision equipment uses thermal imaging. It does not magnify light, but rather, picks up the heat given off by people and objects. Cooler objects, like trees or walls, give off relatively little heat, but the human body is much warmer. This heat shows up as colors (the warmer the heat, the brighter the color), which lets the rescuer know where to find the person he is seeking.

FLYING TO THE RESCUE

Two years after Marconi developed radio, the Wright brothers, Orville and Wilbur, invented airplanes. Although airplanes are often

an integral part of a rescue, they were not used regularly until about 1952. They proved to be an excellent way of locating people who had gotten into difficulties in the wilderness.

It is helicopters in particular that play an important role. Strangely enough, Wilbur Wright did not think much of the helicopter—he determined it was "worthless" and said it would never work. He was wrong. Helicopters, and their ability to hover in the air, have saved many lives.

The first practical helicopter, constructed in the United States by Igor Sikorski, did not fly until 1939. Helicopters would later follow airplanes into the work of search and rescue, able to do the jobs that airplanes cannot. Airplanes, for example, need a lot of clear space on the ground in order to take off and land; helicopters can come in to land straight down and take off straight up, and can thus be used in cramped and hard-to-reach places.

Where possible, however, helicopter pilots prefer to land, rather than to hover above the site of an emergency. It is easier to pick up rescuers and load injured people into a helicopter that is firmly on the ground. Landing is also a better way to get a rescue team to the scene of an emergency. If the helicopter cannot land and has to hover, then the team must **rappel** down ropes to the ground, which takes up much more time.

Left: A crewman on a U.S. Coast Guard HH-60J Jayhawk, a medium-range recovery helicopter used for search and rescue, checks the machine's hoist equipment. Although normally stationed onshore, the HH-60J can also take off from a Coast Guard boat.

THE HH60J JAYHAWK HELICOPTER

The Jayhawk helicopter is widely used by the U.S. Coast Guard for search-and-rescue operations, but this is not its only purpose. It is useful, too, in law enforcement, marine environmental protection, and in spotting and stopping drug runners off the U.S. coasts. The Jayhawk also has a military role to play.

Even though it is normally stationed on land, one of the Jayhawk's prime virtues is its ability to land on water. It can take off, too, from 270 ft- and 378 ft-Coast Guard cutters, which act as refuelling and supply points.

The Jayhawks, built by the famous helicopter firm of Sikorski, has a crew of four, can work up to 300 miles from a base station and has a four-hour span of endurance. The helicopters carry an impressive array of high-tech equipment: the Global Positioning System and state-of-the-art radio, radar, and navigational aids. Measuring 64.8 ft in length, it has a 50-ft fuselage, and is driven by two 1800-shp T700-GE-401C turboshaft engines.

Although the Jayhawk's maximum cruising speed at 5,000 ft is between 135 and 140 knots, it is capable of making faster "dashes," reaching up to 180 knots.

Landing is not always possible, of course. Mountain climbers, for instance, often need to be rescued from risky places. Someone needing rescue may be lying at the bottom of a ravine or in a small clearing that is surrounded by trees. Such situations are dangerous for the helicopter because there may not be enough room for its rotors to revolve safely. Sometimes, there is a small piece of ground where a helicopter can land—perhaps at the top of a mountain—but it is so small that the only way the pilot can use it is to make a "one-skid landing." One-skid landings can be dangerous and are used only when absolutely necessary. Helicopters do not have landing wheels, like airplanes; instead, they have skids, or long, flat "feet." In a one-skid landing, the pilot carefully lowers the helicopter down until one skid is touching a small area of the ground.

Rescuers who get in or out of the helicopter when it is in this position have to be careful not to cause bumps or jolts that can upset the controls. It is all-too-easy to upset the balance of a helicopter and cause it to fall off a mountainside and crash.

A U.S. Air Force MC-130 Combat Talon heads for Libreville, Gabon, as part of a rescue mission to recover survivors from a USAF cargo aircraft that crashed in the Atlantic Ocean in September 1997.

WILDERNESS MEDICINE

Medicine, as practiced in the wilderness, is unique in this respect: paramedics, working far from a medical center, do not necessarily have the drugs or equipment they need. Their role is to provide emergency care and do the best for their patients with what they have available at the time.

In a city, hospitals are likely to have all the equipment or drugs needed to care for the injured or ill. Moreover, their patients have usually been brought in for treatment relatively quickly. Out in the wilderness, however, people who have been injured or fallen ill must often wait some time before medical help arrives. They are also out in the open, at the mercy of the weather—heat, cold, rain, even snow and ice. The result is that a person's health and physical condition may have deteriorated by the time a rescue team reaches him or her, and rescue teams must face the fact that someone seriously injured may now be too weak to survive, or may even have died in the meantime.

All this makes wilderness medicine demanding as well as difficult, and **paramedics** train hard to gain the knowledge and skills required. Their priority on an SAR mission is to treat injured people so that it is safe to move them—usually, although not

Left: However dramatic and beautiful this area of the Mexican-American border appears, being injured or ill here can have serious consequences.

In this dramatic and heart-rending scene, a one-year-old child is rescued by a civilian volunteer from floodwaters caused by Hurricane Hortense in Guayama in 1996.

always, by helicopter—to the nearest hospital. In the hospital, they will recover from their injuries, but before they can get there, the paramedics have several important tasks.

Left: A member of the U.S. Air Force's Air Rescue wing treats a role-play "survivor" from a simulated air crash in the Atacama Desert, north of Santiago, Chile.

GETTING OUT OF DANGER

The first thing paramedics must do on arriving at the scene of an emergency is determine whether the danger that initially caused the injury is still there. For example, if someone has been hurt in a rock-fall from a mountain, are there likely to be any more rockfalls that could cause more trouble? If so, the injured person needs to be moved away and out of danger. This, of course, also ensures that the rescuers avoid the danger. If they get injured, too, they will not be able to help anyone and could need rescuing themselves.

Next, paramedics must discover if the accident has caused any damage that is not immediately obvious. Imagine, for instance, that a climber has fallen down a mountain and broken his leg, an obvious-enough injury. He might, however, have also hit his head on a rock when he landed and suffered an injury to the brain—which is much more serious.

Taking a careful look at a patient is an important part of the para-medic's job out in the wilderness. Does the patient seem to be unusually red in the face? This may indicate that she is suffering from a fever or (conversely) that she has succumbed to **hypothermia**. If a patient's face looks rather blue, this is a sign of **cyanosis**, which means there is a lack of oxygen in the blood. A person who has had a heart attack, for example, will be suffering from cyanosis, so a blue face indicates a serious problem for the paramedic.

Is the patient conscious? Even if she is, the paramedic cannot be sure nothing is wrong, and must find out more. Does the patient talk sensibly or is she confused and dazed? Does she feel any pain, and where is it? The answers to such questions can give a better idea of just how bad the patient's injuries are and how best to treat them.

A physical examination—feeling various parts of the body—is important to assess the patient's general condition and find out whether there are any more injuries. This must, of course, be done gently, otherwise the patient may suffer more pain or further damage. For instance, if a paramedic takes off a patient's helmet and finds that the hair underneath seems to be wet and matted, this could be a sign of a fractured skull. There could be pieces of bone at

A man is placed in an SAR vehicle in the Austrian Alps—he is suffering from exposure, a constant danger for climbers.

CODE OF ALERTNESS

In wilderness medicine, medics use an LOC (level of consciousness) code to determine how alert patients are and how orientated (aware of their surroundings) they are. This is known as the LOC A+O code. The highest score is LOC A+O x 4, which means that patients know:

1) Their own name.

2) Where they are.

3) What time it is, at least roughly.

4) About the accident and the injury they have suffered.

If patients know the answer to the first three questions only, the score is LOC A+O x 3. LOC A+O x 2 means they know their name and where they are, but nothing else. LOC A+O x 1 means they know their name, but not the answers to the last three questions.

Naturally, the patient who scores LOC A+O x 4 is in a much better condition than those who score less. A patient's level of awareness thus provides important information about how serious the injuries are.

Right: This is an anxious moment for these U.S. Coast Guard paramedics as they try to revive a man found adrift in a small boat in the Gulf of Mexico by using breathing apparatus. The man survived, due to the excellent treatment he received.

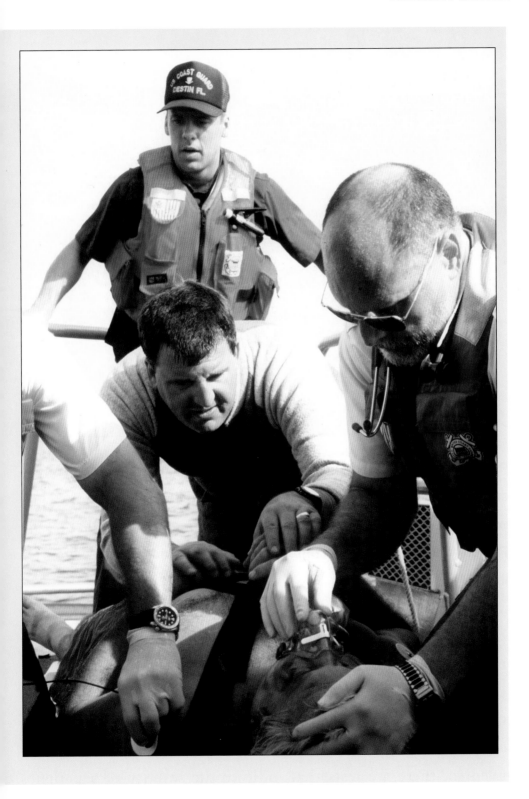

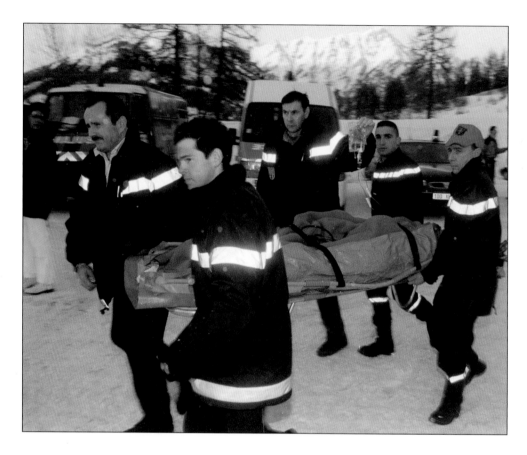

Rescue workers carry a survivor on a stretcher after an avalanche swept away a group of teenagers and their guides who were trekking with snowshoes near the ski resort of Les Orres in the southern French Alps in 2000. Unfortunately, 11 people died, and 19 were injured in the accident.

the site of the fracture, and the paramedic must be careful not to move or disturb them.

In search-and-rescue work, the greatest worry is that patients might die despite all efforts to save their lives. This does happen, of course, because paramedics, like doctors, are not miracle workers. Even so, there are tests that indicate the severity of a patient's

Search-and-rescue training can be tough on canines as well. This dog
is working in the snowbound, icy conditions SAR often involves in
the Rocky Mountains of Colorado.

injuries and whether they are likely to be life threatening, in which case, preventive action can be taken.

THE ABCs OF WILDERNESS MEDICINE

There are five important things to look out for—as easy to remember as A, B, C, D, and E.

A is for Airway: Is the patient's airway open so that he can breathe properly? If not, there might be something in the way—perhaps blood or a "foreign body," such as a piece of chewing gum. Whatever is blocking the airway must be removed. One way to clear an airway is to put a hand on the patient's forehead, push the head back gently, and then lift the chin.

B is for Breathing: Is the patient breathing? If not, the paramedic must perform what is called "rescue breathing." One way of doing this is with mouth-to-mouth resuscitation, in which the paramedic breathes into the patient's mouth to fill his lungs with air. After a while, if all goes well, the patient will start breathing independently.

C is for Circulation: Blood circulates through the body all the time. Taking a patient's pulse, which has a throbbing rhythm, is the way to

February 2000: doctors and rescue workers try to revive an avalanche victim on the Meierhoftal ski slope near Davos, Switzerland.

find out if the circulation is normal. If it is not, this may indicate severe bleeding somewhere in the body.

D is for Disability: It is extremely important to find out if there has been any injury to the spine, the column of small bones that runs down the back starting at the neck. If the spine is injured, the head and neck should not be moved: if they are, the result could be **paralysis**, which means that the patient will lose the ability to move his arms or legs or other parts of his body. If that happens, then the patient could become disabled, perhaps for only a short time, perhaps for life.

E is for Environment: Injuries can sometimes be hidden under the clothes the patient is wearing. It might be a broken bone, a bleeding wound, or severe bruising to the skin. In wilderness medicine, the environment must be taken into consideration because, unlike doctors in hospitals, paramedics usually have to work out-of-doors. In a hospital, most or all of a patient's clothes can be removed without problems. In the wilderness, however, clothes are needed to protect against the cold or wind or against the effects of heat and sun. Paramedics must, therefore, make sure they do not remove much clothing—just enough to let them examine the injury.

WILDERNESS MEDICINE IN HISTORY

Wilderness medicine began around 300 years ago, in 1812, when soldiers in the army of the French emperor Napoleon Bonaparte were first trained to look after those injured in war. Later, in the 19th century, the American West was opened up, and at that time, the West was indeed wild: the only medical care available was wilderness medicine.

As towns and cities expanded across America, so did hospitals. This, however, was not the end of wilderness medicine. After World War II, the wilderness became a place for vacations and adventure. The American Red Cross, which was founded in 1905, taught first aid, but this was not specialized enough to make sure that people injured in the wilderness received the medical treatment they needed. Something better was required.

In 1966, the U.S. government took action and Congress passed the National Highways Safety Act. Under this law, the Department

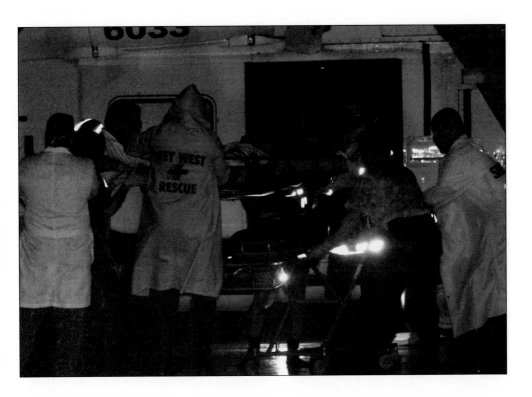

U.S. Coast Guard members rescued this survivor who suffered head injuries in an aircraft crash off the Florida coast in 2000.

of Transportation was required to create and run special Emergency Medical Services (EMS). A year later, in 1967, an important book was published—*Medicine for Mountaineering*, edited by James Wilkerson, a doctor. This was one of the first books to deal with nearly the whole range of medical emergencies that could occur in the wilderness.

After this, there were many opportunities for Americans to learn how to practice wilderness medicine. For example, the first EMT (Emergency Medical Technician) course began in 1976. Special "wilderness first aid" courses started in Conway, New Hampshire, in 1977. The Wilderness Medical Society was founded in 1985. These

Mike Tucker of the Federal Emergency Management Agency (FEMA) Urban SAR Texas Task Force 1 team participates in a winter-acclimatization exercise near Salt Lake City, Utah.

organizations, along with courses and the publication of more wilderness-medicine books, gave visitors and rescue teams valuable skills and information about what to do when things go wrong in the wilderness.

Left: In the Austrian Alps, near the city of Salzburg, a helicopter hovers above rescue personnel near a tunnel where as many as 172 skiers were feared killed in a blazing train wreck near Kaprun in November 2000. Rescue workers were able to free eight passengers trapped deep inside the Kitzenhorn Mountain.

EDUCATION AND TRAINING

Vacations in the wilderness—or the "great outdoors" as it is often called—require careful preparation. For these vacations, at least one person should have some training in not just how to avoid problems, but also how to deal with them.

In the wilderness, there is no electricity supply to depend on, no water supply, no telephone, no roads, and no transportation—you really are on your own. Little wonder, then, that members of USSARTF and other search-and-rescue organizations are eager to pass on the same skills they train so hard to attain themselves. "Education is one of our primary missions," says Steven Labov, Chief of USSARTF. "People should learn how to help themselves out in the wilderness. They need to be wilderness-wise."

HOW NOT TO NEED RESCUING

The USSARTF and other SAR organizations work hard to teach people how to avoid difficulties and help themselves. Several issues are key to ensuring a safe and successful expedition.

Is the leader of the group trained and experienced in wilderness conditions? Is the leader familiar with the area where the group is going to travel?

Left: It is calm now, but these hikers on Hummocks Trail at Mount Saint Helens, Washington, are treading ground once devastated by volcanic eruptions.

Has everyone in the group been checked out for allergies or other medical conditions that might affect them while they are in the more challenging conditions of the wilderness?

Does everyone have the proper clothing to protect them if the weather turns bad?

Is everyone reasonably fit and energetic so that exploring the wilderness will not exhaust them?

Is the group taking enough food and water?

Does the group have a proper first aid kit?

Does the group have good maps of the wilderness area?

Is the group carrying a radio or other means of communication in case they get into trouble?

Has information about the group's itinerary, or route, through the wilderness been left behind with someone who can raise the alarm if necessary?

People who go out into the wilderness on their own must make sure that they can answer "yes" to all of those questions. Yet, answering "yes" does not guarantee that there will be no trouble. Going out into the wilderness is an adventure, and adventures can present some nasty surprises. But at least it is possible to avoid making obvious mistakes.

MANY LESSONS TO LEARN

SAR organizations offer many forms of education. They put on wilderness-survival exhibitions and run training courses on subjects such as first aid. They give talks and demonstrations of survival skills. They write magazine and newspaper articles and run Internet

Congratulations! Two French SAR men shake hands after rescuing hikers trapped by weather in this igloo in the French Alps. Three French hikers, who spent nine days here trapped by weather conditions, used a cellular phone to locate their rescuers.

Web sites to give advice and answer questions.

Many people have rather romantic ideas about the wilderness. For them, the wilderness is the stuff of fairy tales—an ideal place, where they need not expect to face any difficulties. This, of course, is an illusion. All sorts of things can (and do) go wrong—often because people venture into the wilderness without understanding or learning what it is all about.

For one thing, they often fail to take the right sort of clothing and

Steve Lathrop of the Oswego County Pioneer SAR team tells a class about the exploits of his rescue dog Vlux.

equipment. Out in the wilderness, people must rely on themselves, so standard advice includes a surprisingly long list of essential supplies and equipment. Wilderness adventurers must make sure to take enough food and water; to have the proper clothing, like the right boots for walking in rough country; and to take sleeping bags, as well as cutlery and other utensils, for eating meals; creams for protection from the sun; and medications to treat insect bites or cuts. And each person should have a whistle hanging around his or her neck; anyone who gets into difficulties when away from the group can then signal for help.

A common problem in the wilderness is getting lost. It is all-too-easy, for instance, to be exploring a wood and then discover that it is impossible to find a way out, or to be trekking through rough country in a group and then to stop to look at something interesting, during which time the rest of the group disappears. This is a frightening experience, which is where education becomes important.

USSARTF runs a special internet Web site (www.ussartf.org/child_survival_.htm) aimed at children. It features advice on how to

This SAR mountaineering team is well equipped for rescue work occasioned by bad weather or avalanches in the French Alps.

DRESSING FOR THE WILDERNESS

You never know what the weather might do in the wilderness; it changes all the time. A hot day may give way to a cold night; the sun may give way to rain. This makes dressing properly for the wilderness an important part of surviving there.

The secret is to dress in layers—several items of clothing, worn one on top of the other, but none of them so thick that you cannot move easily. The first layer, worn next to your skin, is there to keep you dry. The next is for **insulation**, to help keep you warm by stopping your body heat from escaping. In cold weather, you may need two layers of insulation, and in rain, another layer of clothing to keep you from getting wet. This layer will also keep the wind off and keep you from feeling chilled.

However, the weather is not the only factor to consider when dressing for the wilderness. The type of activity you are doing is also important: a long trek, or hours of climbing up a mountainside, can make you feel hot, which will mean you need less insulation from your clothes. On the other hand, when sitting around the campfire in the evening, you will probably need another layer of clothing to keep warm.

make your own survival kit, what to do if you find yourself still lost when it gets dark, how to make it easy for rescuers to see you, and how to keep warm on cold conditions. Such knowledge will help children cope with what is an extremely frightening, and also unexpected, experience.

In a helicopter high above the scene, FEMA Director Joe Allbaugh surveys flood damage in the forests around Kimball, West Virginia, in 2001.

ORIENTEERING

Adults must also learn survival skills, for they, too, can (and do) get lost. This is what makes **orienteering** such an important subject in wilderness education. Orienteering simply means using a map and a compass to find your way. The map shows the features of the wilderness—mountains or hills, valleys, rivers or lakes, or long stretches of scrubland. The compass shows the direction to follow—north, south, east, west, or points in between. If used properly, the map

Stephanie Kelley at the helm of a U.S. Coast Guard 41-foot (12-m) utility boat, watched by Petty Officer 2nd Class Bill Pierce. Stephanie was lucky enough to win a competition that allowed her to train for a day with the Coast Guard near Galveston, Texas.

and compass together identify your current position and also how to reach that part of the wilderness where you want to be.

Learning orienteering means first of all learning how a compass works and how to read it. On a compass, the Earth's magnetic field always makes the needle turn toward north; this, however, is not what is called "true" north, which is recorded on ordinary maps. What the compass shows is the "magnetic" north, which is also called "compass" north.

Orienteers use special maps that indicate magnetic, or compass, north by blue or black lines. It is therefore possible to match up the compass reading with what is shown on the map—and then use this information to work out the other compass directions.

Orienteering maps also indicate the different features of a wilderness. Black symbols are used for rock features—cliffs, stony ground, or large boulders. Features running in lines, known as linear features, are also shown in black, and indicate roads, trails, fences, and buildings. Features of the land, or landforms, are shown in brown; these may be contour lines indicating the outlines of small hills, or symbols indicating ditches or banks of earth. Ponds, rivers, streams, and marshes are all water features, and are indicated in blue. Yellow, white, or green is used for vegetation features, such as woods, forests, and meadows.

It is important for orienteers to know if this vegetation will present obstacles along the route. Vegetation shown in white means that there will be little problem in getting through it. Yellow means that the way is reasonably clear. If it is not, the vegetation is shown in green—and if dark green is used, it will be impossible to get through it.

PRACTICE MAKES PERFECT

There is a lot of training and practice to be done before newly learned wilderness skills can be used for real. For example, before going out into the wilderness, you could test your orienteering skills by navigating around a large park. Children are taught to practice getting around their own bedrooms at home with the light off. The

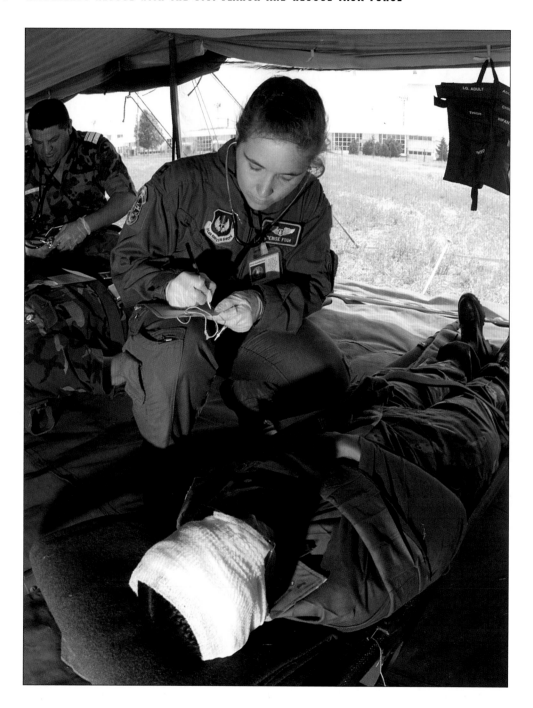

Flight nurse Captain Denise Fogh from the U.S. Air Force carries out basic health checks on a simulated injured patient during Exercise Rescue Eagle in Romania, 2000.

Search-and-rescue personnel retrieve a wilderness visitor who got into difficulties in a river near Pulaski, New York State.

point of this exercise is to learn the importance of taking note of your surroundings while there is still daylight—useful for a child lost in the woods at night.

Another way of testing orienteering and other wilderness skills is to go on a course that gives you a taste of what the wilderness is like. The Canadian organization, Advance Response Training (ART), for example, arranges for groups to go out into the wilderness on a trial run for a few days and nights. Trained wilderness experts go along, too, but even so, people have to do everything for themselves. They must make their own fires and gather the materials to build a shelter for sleeping in at night. They also learn how to track and catch small animals or birds for food and about wild plants, learning which ones are safe to eat and which ones to avoid.

But getting a wilderness education is not just about learning what the wilderness is like and what to do there. Most importantly, it is about gaining confidence when in wilderness surroundings, which, in turn, makes being there enjoyable. However, education can also have another, quite different effect. It can get rid of any illusions people might have about the wilderness. The wilderness does not suit everyone. For some people, it is too rough and uncomfortable; others may find the physical challenges of walking, climbing, carrying loads, or simple exposure to the wind and the rain too difficult. The "great outdoors" might seem like a good idea from the safety and warmth of home, but out there, the reality is different. If they learn nothing else from their training, such people realize it is probably better for them to forget about the wilderness.

Most of all, education about the wilderness provides this lesson: that venturing into it and surviving there is all about "togetherness," taking care of each other, sharing food or equipment, and, if necessary, rescuing each other. Even if they have never met before, the members of a group become a team, and each has a part to play in making time spent in the wilderness a great experience.

Right: A dog and his search and rescue trainer rehearse rescue work over wintry, muddy ground in a wood in Ohio.

WILDERNESS RESCUE IN THE 21ST CENTURY

Search and rescue has consistently taken advantage of emerging technology, and this will continue in the 21st century. There always will be new ways of locating people and new means of communication. The roles of computers and the Internet grow, and rescue robots help people trapped in hard-to-reach places.

One of the biggest problems of the wilderness is the enormous size of the area that must be searched during an SAR mission. However, airlines routinely fly planes over wilderness areas during their journeys from one city to another—and they can help. In the 21st century, experts hope that airplanes could be fitted with Global Positioning Systems (GPS) to pick up the positions of people in the wilderness and send the information back to search-and-rescue organizations. Also under development are Personal Locator Beacons (**PLBs**), which can be carried by individual travelers. Any difficulties, and it will be easy enough to signal for help.

Helicopters and aircraft are already used, but will become more efficient than ever when equipped with night-vision technology. Search-and-rescue operations can be a race against time, because searches currently stop when night falls or when weather conditions

Left: Rescuers walk in the heavy snow on a mountain where climbers have disappeared in the Italian Alps, 1999. Harsh weather conditions can often make rescue operations difficult and hazardous.

The Federal Emergency Management Agency (FEMA) is an extremely powerful force in the United States. Created by a Presidential Executive Order, FEMA is always there with aid, advice, and assistance for any problem—whether it involves drugs, urban riots, or SAR operations.

make it too dark to continue. Night-vision technology can change all that; the sun may set, but the search can go on.

FASTER LOCATION, FASTER RESCUE

People in the wilderness could also be located by satellites that orbit the Earth. There is already a search-and-rescue satellite system (SARSAT) that uses satellites in orbit close to the Earth and stationary satellites. It is possible that, in time, there will be a world-wide search-and-rescue Internet link to these satellites. By this means, calls for help would be sent to rescue control centers, and two-way communications could enable rescuers to get more information from the people needing rescue.

A British invention, the **hovercraft**, will help speed up rescues.

A Canadian Coast Guard rescue hovercraft near Vancouver, British Columbia. Built in Britain, the CG-045 has been used by the Canadian Coast Guard since the 1970s.

The first hovercraft traveled across the English Channel in 1959. Since then, it has been used in many countries as passenger transporation. In the 21st century, however, hovercraft could find a new role in search and rescue. At the moment, hovercraft can travel over waterways or rough ground, but operate best over relatively short distances. The new hovercraft will be able to travel over much longer distances, at higher speeds. They could be equipped to work like vertical takeoff and landing (**VTOL**) aircraft—in other words,

An FBI emergency response team searches the crash site of a Gulfstream corporate jet near Aspen in Colorado, 2001. The use of helicopters makes search-and-rescue operations in inaccessible mountain areas much easier.

able to land straight down onto the ground and take off again straight up.

This would be useful for SAR emergencies in narrow, difficult-to-reach places, such as **ravines**. Sometimes, however, the rescue area is

THE STORY OF SARSAT

The idea for Search and Rescue Satellites (**SARSAT**) began with a tragedy in 1970, when an aircraft with two members of the U.S. Congress on board crashed in an unknown area in Alaska. In spite of tremendous efforts to locate the aircraft, nothing was ever found.

After this, Congress decided that all U.S. aircraft must carry an Emergency Locator Transmitter (ELT). In the event of a crash, the transmitter immediately sends out a homing signal to lead rescuers to the site. ELTs were eventually replaced by a system of more effective earth-orbiting satellites.

This was the start of the SARSAT system, which was developed by the United States, Canada, and France. It had its own **waveband**, which was used only for SAR emergencies. The Soviet Union developed a satellite system of its own, known as **COSPAS**. In 1979, the two systems were combined, and became known as **COSPAS-SARSAT**. The first joint satellite was launched in 1982, and the system began operating two years later.

Today, it includes 25 more countries and has 28 ground stations and 15 control organizations located around the world. In its first 20 years, the COSPAS-SARSAT system has enabled 12,889 people to be rescued, 4,302 in the United States alone.

so difficult to reach that even VTOL hovercraft cannot land there. Setting up a column of air to lift injured people up into the rescue vehicle as it hovers above the ground could solve this problem. The latest technological developments suggests that it may be possible for new hovercraft to be jet-propelled and be able to travel faster than the speed of sound, just as the Concorde airliner does today.

ATOMIC VEHICLES AND OTHER ADVANCES

Vehicles that run on atomic power (APVs) could be used in 21st-century search and rescue. These would have a big advantage over conventional vehicles, which need frequent refueling. An atomic vehicle would probably be able to operate for as long as it was

In war-torn Mozambique, southwestern Africa, Red Cross personnel use telephone satellite equipment to aid in emergency medical and relief efforts.

In 2000, at a contest in Osaka, Japan, rescue robots compete with each other to find dolls representing real-life disaster victims. This type of technology could become common in rescue operations in the future.

When the World Trade Center collapsed after the 2001 terrorist attack, members of the California Task Force-3, who are normally involved in wilderness search-and-rescue operations, helped clear away the wreckage and search for survivors.

needed to complete a rescue—days rather than hours. In this case, the vehicles would also be "homes" for the rescuers, equipped with all they needed to stay out in the wilderness for long periods of time.

The communicators used in search and rescue will be smaller and

ROBOTS AT THE WORLD TRADE CENTER

When the twin towers of the World Trade Center in New York City collapsed after the terrorist attacks of September 11, 2001, robots played their part in the work of search and rescue. Human searchers could not penetrate the enormous mass of twisted steel and concrete covered in thick dust—and it was extremely dangerous. The robots were not bothered, of course. They went deep into the wreckage, guided by remote control.

Able to move in any direction, the robots were equipped with many different instruments that enabled them to detect trapped victims. They carried infrared cameras to send back pictures of what the wreckage was like inside. They had "biological" sensors to find people who were trapped. Voice-activated microphones picked up cries for help. Video screens enabled the rescuers outside to see where it was safe for them to enter and work their way through the wreckage.

Of course, the robots did not replace the human rescuers. What they did do was enable them to search much further than they could have done on their own and helped to reduce the risk that the rescuers, too, would become victims of the worst disaster the United States has ever suffered.

more convenient to use. Most of them will form a part of the rescuer's clothing: antennas (for picking up radio signals) could be easily sewn into a shirt or jacket.

Already used in search-and-rescue operations, robots will be

U.S. Navy, U.S. Air Force, and Guam civilian rescue workers extract a young survivor from the wreckage of crashed Korean Airlines Flight 801. The aircraft had crashed in August 1997 in Guam, South America, and the United States immediately sent rescue teams to offer medical assistance.

programmed to do many more tasks. The size of a robot depends on the job to be performed. Suppose a **potholer** is trapped inside a cave; whether or not he is injured, he is in a dangerous situation, especially if it is likely to take some time for rescuers to reach him. There is a narrow tunnel leading to the place where the potholer is trapped, but it is too small for a person to get through. A robot of the right size could be sent instead, carrying air, food, or medicine to make the potholer more comfortable and keep him alive until the rescuers are able to reach him.

Other robots can help in the rescue itself. For example, if the ceiling of an escape route is in danger of falling down, a robot could be used to hold it up, enabling rescuers to get through and reach the trapped potholer and take him to safety.

Sometimes, it might be difficult for rescuers to find out exactly where the trapped potholer is. New instruments will be able to detect the position of life-forms in a mass of rock; this will make rescue much quicker. The potholer, too, may be carrying his own instrument, a **MONCOM**. Worn around the wrist, like a watch, but also small enough to fit into a pocket, the MONCOM is a monitor/communicator that shows vital life signs, such as pulse rate, temperature, or breathing. It can transmit this important information to the rescuers so that they know what sort of condition the potholer is in. Knowing this in advance means that the team can give the right treatment as soon as they reach the trapped potholer.

Of course, not all these technological advances will be introduced into the work of search and rescue at the same time. It could take up to 50 or even 100 years before some of them can be used. Others, such as rescue robots or satellite systems, which are already used today, will be improved to perform even more jobs—not just in the 21st century, but beyond. There is no end to the advance of technology and what it can do to make search and rescue easier, safer, faster—and more successful.

GLOSSARY

Altruistic: to do good for the sake of others without expecting personal reward

COSPAS: Soviet search-and-rescue satellite system; see COSPAS-SARSAT

COSPAS-SARSAT: the system created in 1979 by combining the COSPAS and SARSAT search-and-rescue systems

Cyanosis: a discoloration of the skin caused by lack of oxygen

Dehydrating: where the body lacks water, leading to weakness and eventually illness

GPS: Global Positioning System; the satellite system that makes it possible to locate anyone anywhere on earth

Hovercraft: a vehicle that travels across both land and sea on a cushion of air

Hypothermia: abnormally low body temperature, induced by exposure to cold weather

Insulation: a layer (or layers) of material or clothing that stops body heat from escaping into the atmosphere

Litter: the basket that attaches to a helicopter winch to safely hold injured people

MONCOM: monitor and communicator

Orienteering: the method of finding the way from one place to another by using a map and compass; it is also the name of a sport, in which contestants race on foot from one checkpoint to another—all found with the aid of a map and compass

Outback: the remote bush country of Australia's interior

Paralysis: a loss, or partial loss, of the ability to move a part of the body

Paramedic: a person who supplements the work of the medical profession, but is not a doctor

PLBs: personal locator beacons—instruments that enable people to send a signal indicating where they are

Potholer: someone who explores underground caves and waterways

Rappel: to slide down ropes from a helicopter to fight fires

Ravine: a deep, narrow, steep-sided valley (usually caused by the action of running water)

SARSAT: Search and Rescue Satellite system used in the United States, Canada, and France

Scrubland: an area of arid land, where only stunted trees, bushes, and other plants can grow

VTOL: Vertical Takeoff and Landing; a system letting aircraft take off and land vertically

Waveband: a range of wavelengths or frequencies used for a particular type of radio transmission

VHF/FM: radion abbrevation for Very High Frequency/Frequency Modulation

CHRONOLOGY

1876: Telephone invented by Alexander Graham Bell.

1901: First radio message sent by Guglielmo Marconi.

1903: Orville and Wilbur Wright fly the first heavier-than-air aircraft (Flyer I).

1905: The American Red Cross is founded.

1939: First successful helicopter invented by Igor Sikorski.

1959: Mountain Rescue Association (MRA) is established; hovercraft is invented in Britain by Christopher Cockerell.

1966: National Highways Safety Act (United States); first flight of the first operational VTOL aircraft—a Harrier "jump jet" flown by Britain's Royal Air Force.

1967: Publication of *Medicine for Mountaineering*, edited by James Wilkerson.

1970: Military Assistance to Safety and Traffic (MAST) established in the United States to provide helicopters as ambulances in search-and-rescue operations; aircraft crash in Alaska leads to the setting up of SARSAT.

1977: First Wilderness EMT (Emergency Medical Technician) course starts at the University of Virginia; wilderness first-aid courses started by the Stonehearth Open Learning Opportunities (SOLO) at Conway, New Hampshire.

1979: The Soviet Union, together with United States, Canada, and France, establishes the COSPAS-SARSAT satellite search-and-rescue system.

1982: First COSPAS-SARSAT Earth-orbiting satellite launched.

1984: COSPAS-SARSAT system fully operational; SOLO develops first Wilderness First Responder (First Aid) set of training courses.

1985: First Wilderness First Responder (First Aid) course started in Florida.

1999: United States Search and Rescue Task Force established.

2001: September 11, robots used to search the wreckage of the World Trade Center, New York after terrorist attacks.

FURTHER INFORMATION

USEFUL WEB SITES

United States Search and Rescue Task Force (USSARTF): www/ussartf.org

Advance Response Training (ART, Canada): www.artraining.on.ca

USSARTF: Child Survival Education: www.ussarft.org/child_survival_.htm

Orienteering Map: www.williams/edu/Biology/orienteering/map.html

What is Orienteering? www.williams.edu/Biology/orienteering/o~index.html

Rescue Training Resource Guide: www.techrescue.org

National Search and Rescue Committee (NSARC)—U.S. Coast Guard: www.uscg.mil/hq/g-o/g-opr/nsarc/nsarc.htm

Search and Rescue Satellites (SARSAT): www.osdpd.noaa.gov:8080/SARSAT/homepage.html; www.sarsat.noaa.gov

FURTHER READING

Bulanda, Susan. *Ready to Serve! Ready to Save!: Strategies of Real-Life Search and Rescue Missions.* Wilsonville, Oregon: Doral Publishing Inc., 1999.

Green, Michael. *Air Rescue Teams.* Monkato, MN: Capstone Press, 2000.

Keller, William. *Keller's Outdoor Survival Guide: How to Prevail When Lost, Stranded, or Injured in the Wilderness.* Minocqua, Wis: Willow Creek Press, 2001.

Setnicka, Tom. *Wilderness Search and Rescue.* Boston, Massachusetts: Appalachian Mountain Club, 1980.

Tilton, Buck. *The Basic Essentials of Rescue from the Back Country.* Merrillville, Indiana: ICS Books, Inc., 1991.

ABOUT THE AUTHOR

Brenda Ralph Lewis is a prolific writer of books, articles, television documentary scripts, and other materials on history, royalty, military subjects, aviation, and philately. Her writing includes many books on ancient history, culture, and life and books on World War II: *The Hitler Youth: The* Hitlerjugend *in Peace and War 1933–1945* (2000), *Women At War* (2001), and *The Story of Anne Frank* (2001). She has also written or contributed to numerous books for children, including *The Aztecs* (1999), *Stamps! A Young Philatelist's Guide* (1998), and *Ritual Sacrifice: A History* (2002). She lives in Buckinghamshire, England.

INDEX

References in italics refer to illustrations